Quiet Reflections
of
God

Elaine Koenig Krome

Fairway Press
Lima, Ohio

QUIET REFLECTIONS OF GOD

FIRST EDITION
Copyright © 2008 by
Elaine Krome

Scripture quotations are from the *Holy Bible*, *New International Version*. Copyright © 1973, 1978, 1984 International Bible Society. Used by permission of Zondervan Bible Publishers. All rights reserved.

Library Of Congress Control Number: 2007943117

ISBN-13: 978-0-7880-2208-1
ISBN-10: 0-7880-2208-3

PRINTED IN U.S.A.

Dedicated to the glory of God

Contents

Acknowledgments

The development and completion of this work has been a journey of four years. The project began as a simple historical document of the windows, but as time went on the Holy Spirit guided the writing in a total new direction. Many people have contributed time and effort to this endeavor. Hugh Kluttz, Tracey Lederer, Patti Lloyd, Wendy Roberts, Ginny Scobie, and Mary Lib Whelan are among the many who offered their gifts and talents to support this project. My husband, Ron, through his love and support encouraged me to "get it done!" when at times the task seemed overwhelming.

Francis of Assisi once said: "Preach the Gospel at all times. If necessary, use words." The stained-glass pictures are a powerful message of God's love and compassion for His people. May God richly bless you through this art and bring you peace and joy.

Prologue

The congregation of Cross and Crown, Matthews, North Carolina, is very fortunate to have stained-glass windows in their worship space. Individually, the windows tell a story; collectively, they provide another way of listening to God.

Through the beauty of these windows, the rich story of the church is told both in the Old and New Testaments as well as the historical Reformation. Further, the story of Cross and Crown Lutheran Church itself is reflected in the details, colors, and style of each work of art.

The purpose of this book is to help viewers experience the windows in reflection and contemplation. Stained-glass windows are not only historical expressions of faith and beauty, but tools for spiritual encounters in our lives.

Each window takes time. As we look at the windows, we must stay quietly before it. The term "stay" is used because one may be meditating on the windows, through this book at home, or sitting quietly in the sanctuary. There is no right or wrong way to look. Each person will see and understand many different things. The more we study each piece of glass, the more we will begin to see those different aspects. God is always there to help us listen and learn.

This book may be used as a group or individual devotion. Each window includes a review of the subject matter. Meditative thoughts and hymn suggestions may be helpful to focus on the beauty of God's Word through art.

Elaine Koenig Krome

History of Stained Glass in Churches

Stained glass has been used in churches for thousands of years, and the windows created number in the hundreds of thousands. Many have been lost over the years due to such occurrences as fires, wars, vandals, and religious reformation. But enough windows remain to tell the fascinating history of this unique art form.

The earliest use of glass to ornament church windows dates well before written historical records. In the sixth century, St. Gregory had the windows of St. Martin Church in Tours, France, glazed with colored glass. Historical documents indicate that glasswork was mainly used to provide the church with light and protection from the elements, therefore glass was undecorated and mounted in wood, stone, or metal frames.

The earliest known stained-glass images were based on Christian themes. The changing figure of Jesus Christ through various eras illustrates the development of stained glass in history. The scriptures do not describe the physical appearance of Jesus, so the purpose of medieval religious art was to create a visual symbol that would draw viewers into the liturgy.

The earliest existing painted image of the head of Christ dates from around 1050 and is now located in the Musee de l'Oeuvre Notre Dame in Strasbourg, France. Another outstanding image of Christ is found in the east window of St. Peter's Cathedral, Poitiers, France. Dating from around 1160, this incredible window shows Christ with deep blue hair and a body of pale violet on a bright red cross.

In the late twelfth and early thirteenth centuries, stained glass underwent a major transformation. Structural designs made it possible to provide much larger window openings, which were transformed into walls of color and light. Stained glass was no longer a decoration but rather an essential part of the building.

Also in this era, stained glass was built in the theological groundwork laid by Abbot Suger at the Abbey of St. Denis, north of Paris. Inspired by the belief that visible things reveal the invisible, Suger attested that natural light mirrors the light of God.

While Abbot Suger was commissioning more colorful stained-glass windows, an alternative movement was pushing for the elimination of color in church windows. The Cistercian order of monks, which preached the virtues of austerity and simplicity, issued a decree in 1134 proclaiming, "Let windows be of clear glass, without crosses or pictures." Another announcement came in 1182: "Stained glass windows are to be replaced within the space of two years, otherwise the abbot, prior, and cellarer are henceforth all to fast on bread and water every sixth day until they are replaced."

Whether considerable stained glass was destroyed as a result of this rule is unknown, but a window style called *grisaille* (painted gray) evolved in response to the Cistercian rule. These light-filled windows possessed a quiet beauty that contrasted with the more colorful windows.

Over the thirteenth and fourteenth centuries, significant changes took place in the portrayal of religious figures. The influence of the Franciscans helped shift religious art toward more realistic depictions of human beings. The humanization of Christ in art took place over decades, and Christ's portrayal in stained glass gradually became less distant and severe, becoming tender, gentle, and heroic.

By the fifteenth century, Christ was more often portrayed as the Son of Man. This development led to many portrayals of the suffering Christ, and Christ's passion was a prevalent subject. The image of Christ continued to evolve during the Renaissance, and as the period progressed, images of Christ's suffering gave way to an emphasis on his perfect humanity.

A second trend toward increasingly accurate anatomy and realism posed more problems for stained-glass artists in comparison to canvas painters. Increasing realism also made stained glass less suitable as an architectural art. Due to the viewers distance, in a large church, a *clerestory* window may be so high that real-life features and emotions could not been seen.

The Protestant Reformation brought further changes to stained glass. Hundreds of windows were destroyed for their perceived idolatry, and the new windows in Protestant churches depicted historical themes and not religious imagery. It was also felt that colored light in a church emphasized mystery, but religious focus in the period had moved toward preaching and scripture.

For nearly two centuries stained glass was in decline. The methods for making colored glass were neglected and the techniques of the art surrounding the creation of stained-glass images were rarely practiced. In the nineteenth century, however, the revival of interest in all things from the medieval period spurred an effort to recreate the art of stained glass.

Because the Gothic Revivalists placed a great deal of energy into reconstructing, understanding, and preserving medieval stained glass, they managed to rediscover many of the techniques of medieval window builders. *Pietism* also influenced religious art toward sentimentality, and the image of Jesus in the nineteenth century became the gentle Savior, with soft features and a sad expression.

Also during this time, endless reuse of the same images and techniques of mass production reduced stained glass to a "religious art product," rather than a practiced art and craft. One dissenter of this movement was British designer William Morris. Morris and his fellow artists introduced naturalism and beautiful figures into the designs and reestablished the lead lines as a vital part of the overall design. It is from this movement that much of the modern stained-glass art is woven.

Louis Comfort Tiffany, a technical innovator in glass manufacturing, was inspired by the natural world. He used textured and iridescent glass for his works for private homes, but when he entered the world of ecclesiastical art, he found much resistance over both his approach to the subject matter and the type of glass he used. He met opposition to his pastoral landscapes being accepted as church windows except with the Baptists, Unitarians, and Congregationalists. In designing windows for churches, Tiffany carefully selected symbolic flowers and vines interwoven with the light-filled scenery.

Art in the twentieth century has been shaped by many factors — artistic, historical, and social. The different movements in abstract art have had a profound effect on stained glass. Many of the twentieth-century images of Christ portray him as a man of sorrows, presenting an image of Christ the Redeemer.

Father Marie-Alain Couturier, a French Dominican priest and leading light of the Sacred Art movement of the 1930s, was influential in the modern development of stained glass. He believed that all great art was holy and connected to the creativity of God. This belief set the theological stage for contemporary art, which is increasingly abstract and personal, to find a place in houses of worship.

The terrible wars of the first part of the century had a significant effect on art and the church. During World Wars I and II, thousands of churches and cathedrals were destroyed and subsequent generations had a hunger for the new. This especially affected postwar Germany and the extensive rebuilding program was dictated by unspoken guidelines that the new buildings must be constructed with new materials and new concepts in art. Statistics state that the number of new churches built in Germany in the twenty years between 1950 and 1970 was greater than the number built in the 400 years between 1545 and 1945.

Current artwork is often a reflection or interpretation of Christian history, theology, or particular beliefs. These expressions, no matter what style, evoke the presence of Christ in, of, and for the viewer.

East Wall Window

The large diamond-shaped window positioned above the altar on the East Wall is divided into four equal parts, each reflecting the heart of our Christian heritage and beliefs.

Nativity

The Nativity is depicted in the upper left hand section. The manger, or crèche, overflowing with straw is a visual reminder of Jesus' humble birth in a cattle stall. His birth was foretold in Isaiah 7:14: "Therefore the Lord himself will give you a sign; Look, the young woman is with child and shall bear a son, and shall name him Immanuel."

The Chi Rho symbol, an ancient monogram of Christ, rests in the manger.

In the background are the cross and the six-pointed star, formed by superimposing one equilateral triangle on another. The star is classified as the Creator's star, which symbolizes the six days of creation, and is also used in Judaism as the Star of David and the symbol of Zionism.

Baptism

The upper right hand corner reflects three symbols of the Sacrament of Baptism. One of the earliest and most frequent representations of the Holy Spirit is the descending dove. The basis for depicting the Holy Spirit with a dove is found in the stories of Jesus' baptism where all four gospels include a similar event as that described in Mark 1:10-11, "And just as he was coming up out of the water, he saw the heavens torn apart and the Spirit descending like a dove on him. And a voice came from heaven, saying, You are my Son, the Beloved; with you I am well pleased." Jesus' baptism is also recorded in Matthew 3:13-17, Mark 1:9-11, and John 1:29-34.

More than 400 various shapes of the cross exist. This window reflects the cross with a nimbus (a light that surrounds sacred persons or symbols), which indicates that the Holy Spirit is the third Person of the Trinity. St. Paul refers to Baptism in Titus 3:5, calling it "the water of rebirth and renewal in the Holy Spirit."

The shell with several drops of water symbolizes the baptism of Jesus, as well as our own.

Resurrection

The lower left window depicts the Resurrection. St. Paul wrote of the resurrection of the body in 1 Corinthians 15:43: "It is sown in dishonor, it is raised in glory. It is sown in weakness, it is raised in power."

One of our best-loved symbols for death and resurrection is the butterfly.

> The butterfly symbolizes the awakening of life — the symbol of loving care that our Father, let's us fly — free and gently into life — spreading our wings to tell the Good News: Christ is risen, Christ is risen, indeed.
>
> — E. Krome

Plants are also excellent symbols of the Resurrection. The Easter lily is a flower of extraordinary beauty and its white color symbolizes purity. It is a glorious flower emerging from a seemingly dead bulb (grave) to a trumpet-like bloom, heralding the Resurrection.

Communion

The Sacrament of Holy Communion is embraced in the lower right window. The sacrament that Jesus instituted on the evening before his death is known by various names: the Lord's Supper, Holy Eucharist, Holy Communion, and the Breaking of Bread.

Shown on this window are the wheat and grapes, products from which the bread and wine are derived. The chalice, or cup, is inscribed with the letters *I H S*, an abbreviation of a Greek word meaning Jesus.

Reflection

As one stays before the window, the light floods in and the bright vivid colors are a source of strength and peace. At night, illuminated from within, the same sense of strength and reassurance floods the soul. How blessed we are to have such an awe-inspiring, humbling reminder of our past, our present, and our future. This window also serves as a witness to the community, proclaiming the foundations of our faith in the Triune God and revealing our source of hope and meaning.

Hymns

Away In The Manger (LBW #67)
1. Away in the Manger, no crib for his bed,
   The little Lord Jesus laid down his sweet head;
   The stars in the sky looked down where he lay,
   The little Lord Jesus asleep on the hay.

2. The cattle are lowing; the poor baby wakes,
   But little Lord Jesus no crying he makes.
   I love you, Lord Jesus; look down from the sky
   And stay by my cradle till morning is nigh.

3. Be near me, Lord Jesus; I ask you to stay
   Close by me forever and love me, I pray.
   Bless all the dear children in your tender care
   And fit us for heaven to live with you there.

Christ the Lord Is Risen Today; Alleluia! (LBW #128)

1. Christ the Lord is ris'n today; Alleluia!
   Christians, hasten on your way; Alleluia!
   Offer praise with love replete, Alleluia!
   At the paschal victim's feet, Alleluia!

2. For the sheep the Lamb has bled. Alleluia!
   Sinless in the sinner's stead Alleluia!
   Christ the Lord is ris'n on high; Alleluia!
   Now he lives, no more to die. Alleluia!

3. Hail, the victim undefiled, Alleluia!
   God and sinners reconciled, Alleluia!
   When contending death and life, Alleluia!
   Met in strange and awesome strife. Alleluia!

4. Christians, on this holy day, Alleluia!
   All your grateful homage pay; Alleluia!
   Christ the Lord is ris'n on high; Alleluia!
   Now he lives, no more to die. Alleluia!

Let Us Break Bread Together (LBW #212)

1. Let us break bread together on our knees;
   Let us break bread together in our knees.
   When I fall on my knees, with my face to the rising sun,
   O Lord, have mercy on me.

2. Let us drink wine together on our knees;
   Let us drink wine together on our knees.
   When I fall on my knees, with my face to the rising sun,
   O Lord, have mercy on me.

3. Let us praise God together on our knees;
   Let us praise God together on our knees.
   When I fall on my knees, with my face to the rising sun,
   O Lord, have mercy on me.

St. Peter

Dr. Alexander Whyte states in his book, *Bible Characters*, "The four gospels are full of Peter. After the name of our Lord Himself, no name comes up so often as Peter's name. No disciple speaks so often and so much as Peter. Our Lord speaks oftener to Peter than to any other of His disciples: sometimes in praise sometimes in blame. No other disciple ever so boldly confessed, acknowledged and encouraged Jesus as repeatedly as Peter did, and no one ever intruded, interfered and tempted Him as repeatedly as Peter. Jesus spoke words of approval, praise and blessing to Peter but in the same breath, He said harder things to Peter than He ever said to the other twelve, unless it was to Judas."

Although we know him as Peter, the name given to him by Jesus, his birth name was Simon (Mark 3:16). From the time of the Maccabees, "Simon" was one of the most common Jewish names. There are nine Simons in the New Testament and two among the twelve apostles. Peter, a descriptive Greek name, means "the man of rock." A fisherman and brother of Andrew, Peter is the only apostle named as having a wife, but not the only one among the twelve who was married (1 Corinthians 9:5).

Peter was the first to say that Jesus is "the Christ, Son of the living God" (Matthew 16:16) yet it was Peter who denied knowing Jesus three times "before the cock crow[ed] twice" (Mark 14:72).

Two keys that are crossed, forming the letter X, usually symbolize Simon Peter. This image refers to Jesus' promise to give Peter "the keys of the kingdom of heaven" (Matthew 16:19) in addition to symbolizing the spiritual authority of the church (Matthew 18:18).

Peter probably died a martyr's death in Rome at the end of Nero's reign. It has been said that he felt he was unworthy to die on the cross in the same manner as Jesus, so he requested that the cross be inverted.

Reflection

Peter's relationship with Jesus teaches us about the spiritual highs and lows of Christian discipleship. Our faith, like Peter's, may waver, but discipleship means losing our lives as they are and living instead for the sake of the Good News. When have we embodied the prophetic role of ministry by boldly proclaiming through our words and deeds that Jesus is "the Christ, Son of the living God"? When have we hidden our faith in Christ or blatantly denied being in relationship with Jesus? What can we learn about the Christian life and discipleship through these experiences?

Hymn

O God, I Love Thee (LBW #491)

1. O God I love thee; not that my poor love
   May win me entrance to thy heav'n above,
   Nor yet that strangers to thy love must know
   The bitterness of everlasting woe.

2. But, Jesus, thou art mine, and I am thine;
   Clasped to thy bosom by thine arms divine,
   Who on the cruel cross for me hast borne
   The nails, the spear, and man's unpitying scorn.

3. No thought can fathom and no tongue express
   Thy griefs, thy toils, thine anguish measureless,

Thy death, O Lamb of God, the undefiled;
And all for me, thy wayward sinful child.

4. How can I choose but love thee, God's dear Son,
   O Jesus, loveliest and most loving one!
   Were there no heav'n to gain, no hell to flee,
   For what thou art alone I must love thee.

5. Not for the hope of glory or reward,
   But even as thyself hast loved me, Lord,
   I love thee, and love thee and adore,
   Who art my King, My God, forevermore.

St. John

The apostle John, known in scripture as James' brother, spent his early life fishing on the Sea of Galilee. Along with James, Jesus included John in witnessing the mystery of the Transfiguration (Matthew 17:1-9), the agony in the Garden of Gethsemane (John 18:1), and the miracle of raising Jairus' daughter (Luke 8:40-56).

Tradition holds that John was the author of the gospel bearing his name and the book of Revelation, in addition to the three epistles of John. The oldest surviving fragment of any gospel, which historians have dated around 130 CE is a tiny piece from the gospel of John that contains the words of Jesus to Pilate: "For this reason I was born, and for this I came into the world, to testify to the truth" (John 18:37).

John's account of the arrest, trial, and death of Jesus includes many details not found in the other gospels. John also uses the word "sign" (John 2:11) instead of "miracle" as written in the other gospels.

The prominence of Jesus' love in John's writings has given him the title "the apostle of love." John uses the term *love* or the definition of Jesus' love for humankind more than eighty times throughout his writings. As Jesus was being crucified, he committed his mother to John's care, knowing that he would love and provide for her.

The serpent flowing out of the common cup is the most frequently used symbol for John, which is taken from an event not recorded in the Bible. Legend holds that the Emperor Domitian made two attempts on John's life. In one, the Emperor ordered John to drink poisoned wine, but before John could do so, the poison disappeared in the form of a snake slithering from the cup.

Reflection

Several authors have written that John was "loving, lowly, patient and good to the end of his days." Tradition has documented that John preached the gospel until his final days, despite his feeble condition. His last words to his fellow disciples: "Little children, love one another." Regardless of our chronological age, we will always remain children of God. How does this spiritual image impact our relationship with the Triune God? How can we grow by loving God fearlessly? Are we able to see the world anew when we look at it through the lens of a child?

Hymn

A New Commandment (WOV #664)

> A new commandment I give to you,
> That you love one another as I have loved you,
> That you love one another as I have loved you.
>
> By this shall people know you are my disciples,
> If you have love for another;
> By this shall people know you are my disciples;
> If you have love for another.

St. James the Less

James, Son of Alphaeus (Clopas), is an apostle remembered only by his name, for there is not a single authentic word in the New Testament as to the life he lived. But to Jesus, this James was more than a name — he was chosen as one of the original twelve. Tradition records that James was a tax collector by trade. He may have been a cousin to Jesus as John 19:25 describes his mother, Mary, who was the sister of Jesus' mother.

Mark refers to him as "James the Less" probably on account of his short height and to distinguish him from James, the son of Zebedee. According to tradition, James the Less, also called The Minor, was thrown from the temple by the Pharisees and was stoned to death by an infuriated mob while he prayed to God to forgive them.

Artists sometimes depict him leaning on a club, another weapon of death, or by the saw with the handle on the top symbolizing the martyr's death.

Reflection

The unassuming, quiet, faithful servant of God accomplishes much of the world's most needed and most blessed work. Jesus calls each of us individually. Many of us are inconspicuous, ordinary people, but we are children of God blessed with the spiritual gifts He has given us. Reflect upon both your gifts and your faith formation. How is God calling you to use your gifts to serve God's kingdom today?

Hymn

Thine Is the Glory (LBW #145)

1. Thine is the Glory, Risen conqu'ring Son;
   Endless is the vict'ry Thou o'er death hast won!
   Angels in bright raiment Rolled the stone away,
   Kept the folded grave clothes where thy body lay.

3. No more we doubt thee, Glorious Prince of life,
   Life is naught without thee; Aid us in our strife;
   Make us more than conqu'rors, Through thy deathless love;
   Bring us safe through Jordan to thy home above.

Refrain:
   Thine is the glory, Risen, conqu'ring Son;
   Endless is the vict'ry Thou o'er death hast won!

St. Simon

Another of Jesus' apostles, Simon, was called "the Zealot" (Luke 6:15). Prior to 70 AD, a Jewish nationalist party known as The Zealots existed. This group, the strictest sect of the rabbinical schools, insisted upon a literal translation of Jewish law. The crimes they committed in the name of patriotism were horrid. Josephus, a Jewish historian, penned much of the writings of the Zealots.

It is debatable whether Simon was actually a member of the Zealots, as very little is known beyond the fact that he became an apostle. Not a single word or deed Simon ever said or did was documented, except we do know that Simon was the successor to James the Just as bishop of Jerusalem. If indeed Simon was a Zealot, a mighty transformation occurred when he went from a fiery patriot to the legion of the Prince of Peace.

While we do not know how Simon met Jesus, we can assume that Simon embodied gifts that enhanced the composition of the ever-growing group of disciples. His development and spiritual growth must have been evident among the other apostles as Simon participated fully in the mission work as Jesus sent them forth two by two (Mark 6:7).

Reflection

The symbol for Simon, a fish on a hook, refers to his success in fishing for followers through the gospel. If a symbol were to be created in your honor, what would it be? How have you served Christ anonymously within God's kingdom? What would you choose to leave as your legacy?

Hymn

Come Down, O Love Divine (LBW #508)

1. Come down, O Love divine; Seek thou this soul of mine
   And visit it with thine own ardor glowing;
   O Comforter, draw near; within my heart appear
   And kindle it, thy holy flame bestowing.

2. Oh, let it freely burn, till worldly passions turn
   To dust and ashes in its heat consuming;
   And let thy glorious light shine ever on my sight,
   And clothe me round, while my path illuming.

3. Let holy charity mine outward vesture be,
   And lowliness become mine inner clothing
   True lowliness of heart, which takes the humbler part,
   And o'er its own shortcomings weeps with loathing.

4. And so the yearning strong, with which the soul will long,
   Shall far out pass the pow'r of human telling;
   No soul can guess his grace till it become the place
   Where in the Holy Spirit makes his dwelling.

St. James

James the Greater, was one of the closest friends of Jesus. This son of Zebedee was a Galilean fisherman in the area of Capernaum and a brother of John. In all four lists of the apostles, James is included among the first three.

James' mother was Salome, a believer who both followed Jesus on his last journey to Jerusalem and stood at the foot of the cross during the crucifixion (Mark 15:40). Salome also came to anoint Jesus' body on the morning of the resurrection (Mark 16:1). In love for her sons she revealed her deepest wish for them: She said to him (Jesus), "Declare that these two sons of mine will sit, one at your right hand and one at your left, in your kingdom" (Matthew 20:21).

As for Zebedee, the husband of Salome and father of James and John, he is mentioned only once, when his sons left and followed Jesus. It is possible that he, being an orthodox Jew, did not share his family's faith in Jesus. This situation may provide the context for Jesus' sharp words about family relationships in Matthew 10:37-39: "Whoever loves father or mother more than me is not worthy of me; and whoever loves son or daughter more than me is not worthy of me; and whoever does not take up the cross and follow me is not worthy of me. Those who find their life will lose it, and those who lose their life for my sake will find it." In His reply, Jesus affirmed that rewards such as she sought were not at his disposal, but were in the hands of God.

Through scripture writings, we know that James had a zest for his calling and a passion for the Christ. "As he [Jesus] went from there, he saw two brothers, James son of Zebedee and his brother John, in the boat with their father Zebedee, mending their nets, and he called them. Immediately they left the boat and their father and followed him."

The three scallop shells represent James' celebrated three pilgrimages to establish the Christian faith in Spain.

Acts, the last scriptural reference to James, documents that he was the first of the apostles to suffer martyrdom. Herod Agrippa had James arrested and sentenced to death. On the way to the place of martyrdom, the officer who had guarded James was so influenced by James' courage and faith that he fell down at the apostle's feet and begged forgiveness for his treatment of the prisoner. James' reply was "Peace, my son, peace to thee, and the pardon of all your faults" (Acts 12:1-2).

Reflection

James was a man of great compassion and approached his call with the same enthusiasm. Do you see yourself with similar qualities or quietly stand for your faith? If a stranger were invited to your home for a meal, would they see religious items such as a Bible or cross? Would a prayer be offered before the meal? Would they experience an environment of peaceful Christian hospitality?

Hymn

Peace, to Soothe Our Bitter Woes (LBW #338)

1. Peace, to soothe our bitter woes, God in Christ on us bestows;
   Jesus bought our peace with God with is holy precious blood;
   Peace in him for sinners found is the Gospel's joyful sound.

2. Peace within the Church still dwells in her welcomes and farewells;
   And through God's baptismal pow'r, peace surrounds our dying hour.
   Peace be with you full and free, now and through eternity.

St. Andrew

The apostles were all very different from each other in personality, temperament, and background. Andrew, a Greek name meaning "manliness," was a fisherman from a family of fishermen residing in Bethsaida (John 1:44). References to Andrew in the gospels are few. He is known by the name, not of his father, but of his brother — "Andrew, Simon Peter's brother" (Mark 1:16). Together, the two brothers became Jesus' first disciples; as they were harvesting fish from the sea, Jesus called them to follow him and become "fishers of people" (Matthew 4:18-20).

Although less prominent in the scriptures than his brother, Andrew was present for the feeding of the five thousand and he was the disciple who communicated to Jesus that "there is a boy here who has five barley loaves and two fish" (John 6:9). It was Andrew who brought his brother, Simon, to Jesus and told him, "We have found the Messiah" (which is translated Anointed) (John 1:41).

Andrew is also present on the Mount of Olives (Mark 13:3-37) when the disciples ask Jesus when the crisis will occur and when Jesus will come again.

According to tradition, Andrew was martyred by being bound to a transverse or x-shaped cross. Today, the flag of Great Britain bears this same style of cross, signifying Scotland's selection of Andrew as its patron saint.

Reflection

Think about being in the presence of Jesus, listening to him preach and teach. His gentle voice flows over you in endless love. He asks you to follow him, and without hesitation you heed the call. What is it about Jesus that draws you to him and compels you to follow him? What does it mean to follow Jesus today?

Hymn

Jesus Calls Us; O'er The Tumult (LBW #494)

1. Jesus calls us; o'er the tumult
   Of our life's wild restless sea,
   Day by day his clear voice sounding
   Saying, "Christian, follow me."

2. As of old St. Andrew heard it
   By the Galilean lake,
   Turned from home and toil and kindred,
   Leaving all for his dear sake.

4. In our joys and in our sorrows,
   Days of toil and hours of ease,
   Still he calls, in care and pleasures,
   "Christian, love me more than these."

5. Jesus calls us! In your mercy,
   Savior, make us hear your call,
   Give our hearts to your obedience,
   Serve and love you best of all.

St. Bartholomew

The full name of this apostle is Nathanael Bartholomew; he is included in the lists of the apostles in Acts and in the three synoptic gospels. He is twice named by John and is on the first list of disciples that responded to the call of Jesus. At first Bartholomew was cautious; he was certain that the remote village of Nazareth was not a place that could produce the Messiah. John 1:45-46 states: Philip found Nathanael [Bartholomew], and said to him, "We have found him of whom Moses in the law and also the prophets wrote, Jesus of Nazareth, the son of Joseph," Nathanael [Bartholomew] said to him, "Can anything good come out of Nazareth?" Philip said to him, "Come and see."

Jesus already knew about Bartholomew before Philip introduced the two. Nathanael [Bartholomew] asked him, "Where did you get to know me?" Jesus answered, "I saw you under the fig tree before Philip called you" (John 1:48). Historically, the fig tree was a place for private prayer, and Jesus understood Bartholomew as a man of high moral character.

Because Bartholomew believed that the Lord knew all about him while under the fig tree, Jesus promised him, "You will see greater things than these ... you will see heaven opened and the angels of God ascending and descending upon the Son of Man" (John 1:50-51). Bartholomew, who possibly realized more of the glory of Christ than any of the other disciples, now would be the recipient of more heavenly revelations.

The artist's rendering of the symbol of St. Bartholomew includes an open book, as it is believed that he was very familiar with ancient scriptures and spent time in study, particularly under the fig tree. A flaying knife symbolizes the way in which he died, under the command of the brother of King Polymus of Armenia.

Reflection

One of the underlying themes of this stained-glass window is the bond of friendship. Philip introduced Bartholomew to Jesus, and as companions together they spread the Good News. Who has been a companion or mentor to you on your spiritual journey? How have you encouraged others on their journeys?

Another theme is the place where he studied scripture and poured out his soul to the Lord, under the fig tree. Do you have a "fig tree" a nook or place for devotion, meditation, and prayer? May the path leading to the fig tree in the garden of your life never be neglected and choked with weeds.

Hymn

You Are The Way (LBW #464)

1. You are the way; through you alone can we the Father find;
   In you, O Christ, has God revealed His heart, his will his mind!

2. You are the truth; your Word alone true wisdom can impart;
   You only can inform the mind and purify the heart.

3. You are the life; the rending tomb proclaims your conqu'ring arm;
   And those who put their trust in you not death nor hell shall harm.

4. You are the way, the truth, the life; Grant us that way to know,
   That truth to keep, that life to win, whose joys eternal flow.

St. Thomas

The apostle Thomas, one of the original twelve, was a Galilean and a fisherman by trade. Thomas was also known as Didymas, the Twin, but it is unclear as to whom his twin was. Thomas is said to have been a dynamic evangelist who traveled as far as China and India.

Thomas is a prominent character in the gospel of John, particularly John 20:24-29. It is recorded that, having been absent for the appearance of the Risen Lord to the disciple's one week prior, he insisted upon physical proof that Jesus has been resurrected from the dead. Jesus later reappeared to the disciples and invited Thomas to touch his hands and his side, which was pierced by a spear after his death (John 19:34). Upon seeing the Risen Lord with his own eyes, Thomas, full of faith, confidently proclaimed "My Lord and my God!" (John 20:28).

The symbol most frequently used for Thomas is a carpenter's square and spear. The square signifies a church in India built by Thomas' own hands, the spear serves as a reminder of his persecution.

Thomas Sunday is traditionally celebrated the Second Sunday of Easter, which is also the eighth day of the Resurrection.

Reflection

Jesus was very gracious and gentle with Thomas, as he is with us. God's gift to us is that he accepts our doubts, but he also provides us with what we need to move from doubt to faith. Doubt plays an important role in our faith. It prevents spiritual stagnation by encouraging us to continually explore our faith on a deeper level. How do you see Thomas' reaction? Can you identify with him? What doubts do you wrestle with? How has God enabled you to joyfully proclaim "My Lord and my God!"?

Hymn

We Walk By Faith And Not By Sight (WOV #675)

1. We walk by faith and not by sight;
   with gracious words draw near,
   O Christ, who spoke as none e'er spoke:
   "My peace be with you here."

2. We may not touch your hands and side,
   nor follow where you trod;
   but in your promise we rejoice,
   and cry, "My Lord and God!"

3. Help then, O Lord, our unbelief;
   and may our faith abound
   to call on you when you are near
   and seek where you are found.

4. That, when our life of faith is done,
   in realms of clearer light
   we may behold you as you are,
   with full and endless sight.

St. Philip

The apostle Philip appears in the synoptic gospels and Acts only as a name on the list of the original twelve, but his is included in several occasions in the gospel of John. In John 1:43, Jesus invites Philip to "follow me."

The Feeding of the Five Thousand is said to have taken place near Philip's hometown of Bethsaida in Galilee. When Jesus was about to perform a miracle and feed the multitude of people with a small amount of food, Jesus asks Philip where to buy food for these people (John 6:5-6). Jesus was testing Philip as he already knew he would perform a miracle in order to reveal that he was the Son of God.

Philip's presence is also recorded during the Last Supper (John 14:8-11) when a group of Greek Jews asked him to introduce them to Jesus (John 12:20-22) and during the prayer meeting after the ascension of Jesus (Acts 1:13-15).

Reflection

Scholars often write that the Feeding of the Five Thousand has many similarities to the Last Supper as both may be interpreted as feeding the spiritual as well as the physical needs of the people. The bread is both the Bread of Life and nourishment for the body. Jesus created the bread to show he was the Son of God. Today, God continues to sustain us with his Word and the Sacraments of Baptism and Holy Communion. What is it that you hunger for spiritually? What meals or gatherings become sacred for you and your loved ones?

Hymn

Break Now the Bread of Life (LBW #235)

1. Break now the bread of life, Dear Lord, to me,
   As one you broke the loaves Beside the sea.
   Beyond the sacred page I seek you, Lord;
   My spirit waits for you, O living word.

2. You are the bread of life, O Lord to me,
   Your holy Word the truth that rescues me.
   Give me to eat and live with you above;
   Teach me to love your truth, for you are love.

St. Matthew

Among the original twelve disciples whom Jesus chose, there was not one of wealth, noble birth, nor one greatly educated. However, it is possible that Matthew had more money and education than the others. Matthew, whose original name, Levi, relating to the priestly or indicated that he was part of the tribe set apart for worship and the service of God (Numbers 3:6).

Prior to his call, Matthew was a tax collector, responsible for the security of the Roman revenue. All who held these positions gained their reward in that they could extort for their own benefit more than the Caesars demanded. For this reason they were known as "leeches." The three moneybags used to symbolize Matthew refer to his profession as a tax gatherer before he became an apostle (Luke 5:27).

Jesus called Matthew right where he was. He approached the tax collector and commanded him to rise and follow (Matthew 9:9). The scriptures indicate that Matthew did this without delay, leaving his business and associates to follow Jesus. Life had provided Matthew an opportunity to celebrate his transformation and to express his gratitude to God.

Reflection

The reaction of Matthew to Jesus' command was truly a sign of a committed believer and follower. Matthew's response resulted in the rebirth of a man and a soul that was touched by God. Even though it was an unknown future for Matthew, he ignored the sacrifice and obeyed and followed his God. How have you taken risks to follow God? When have you opted for safety and security? What transformations has God worked in your life? Celebrate and express your gratitude to God!

Hymn

Jesu, Jesu, Fill Us With Your Love (WOV #765)

1. Kneels at the feet of his friends,
   Silently washes their feet,
   Master who pours out himself for them.

3. Neighbors are wealthy and poor,
   Varied in color and race,
   Neighbors are nearby and far away

4. These are the ones we will serve,
   These are the ones we will love;
   All these are neighbors to us and you.

Refrain:
   Jesu, Jesu, fill us with your love,
   Show us how to serve the neighbors we have from you.

St. Thaddaeus

As the stained-glass windows each reflect a different light, the apostles are made up of greater and lesser lights. Peter, as an example, was as throng as the blazing sun, but Thaddaeus, a softer light light, also had his place in the plans of Christ. Thaddaeus is the only one described as having three names: Judas, son of James (Luke 6:13), Thaddaeus (Mark 3:18), and Lebbaeus, from the Hebrew, *Leb*, representing warmth and tenderness (Matthew 10:3).

Apart from his three names, he is the apostle that asked Jesus a brief question: "Lord, how is it that you will reveal yourself to us and not to the world?" Thaddaeus began his question by calling Jesus, "Lord" (John 14:23), which indicates he was an obedient and devoted disciple.

In the gospels, there is no record of his occupation before he met Jesus or under what circumstances he was called. However, he is always named whenever the twelve apostles are mentioned in the gospels. Inconspicuous yet obedient, he shared in the ministry of Jesus. Thaddaeus is symbolized by a sailboat with the mast in the shape of a cross, referring to his missionary journeys.

Reflection

The quiet, strong, and faithful servant often does some of the greatest and most astounding work. Do you know people who quietly reflect the life of Christ? The humble, obscure service shines forth with God's love and the Great Commission is lived out daily.

Hymn

If You But Trust In God To Guide You (LBW #453)

1. If you but trust in God to guide you
   And place your confidence in him,
   You'll find him always there beside you,
   To give you hope and strength within.
   For those who trust God's changeless love
   Build on the rock that will not move.

3. In patient trust await his leisure
   In cheerful hope, with heart content
   To take whate'er your Father's pleasure
   And all-discerning love have sent;
   Doubt not your inmost wants are known
   To him who chose you for his own.

4. Sing, pray, and keep his ways unswerving,
   Offer your service faithfully,
   And trust his word; though undeserving,
   You'll find his promise true to be.
   God never will forsake in need
   The soul that trusts in him indeed.

---

*Text copyright © *1978 Lutheran Book of Worship*. Used by permission of Augsburg Fortress.

Judas

Judas Iscariot was one of the original twelve apostles of Jesus holding a position of trust and confidence; he was the treasurer of the group. The tragedy was that he took advantage of his status, as documented in the scriptures (John 12:6). The scriptures tell how some of the other apostles were called, but there is no known record of how Judas became one of the twelve.

For offering to deliver Jesus into the hands of the local leaders, Judas received 30 pieces of silver, about $10 in today's monetary world. Only in the gospels of Matthew and Mark is it written that Judas betrayed Jesus with a kiss. In the New International Version it states, "when Judas, who had betrayed him saw that Jesus was condemned, he was seized with remorse and returned the 30 pieces of silver" (Matthew 27:3).

Accounts of Judas' death are varied. One account states that after Judas returned the money and hung himself, the authorities used the money to buy the "Field of Blood" (*Akeldama*). However, Acts 1:18-19 records that Judas bought the field himself and died as the result of a fall, possibly hung on a rope dangling from a tree and then falling into a pit.

Judas' death is different from the other six biblical suicides, in that it is recorded that Satan "entered into him" (John 13:27; Luke 22:3).

Reflection

For many, Judas is one of the more difficult of the original apostles to understand; yet, perhaps we are more like Judas than we care to admit. Is it painful to accept that we, too, betrayed our Lord? What decisions have we made in our lives that later grieved us? One also has to wonder what would have happened had Judas had the opportunity to plead the pain of his tortured mind and soul before Jesus instead of the priests and elders. As God fills each of us with his unconditional love, grace, forgiveness, and mercy, have you come to peace with the past?

Hymn

Just As I Am, Without One Plea (LBW #296)

1. Just as I am, without one plea,
   But that thy blood was shed for me,
   And that thou bidd'st me come to thee,
   O Lamb of God, I come, I come.

2. Just as I am, and waiting not
   To rid my soul of one dark blot,
   To thee, whose blood can cleanse each spot,
   O Lamb of God, I come, I come.

3. Just as I am, though tossed about
   With many a conflict, many a doubt,
   Fightings and fears within, without,
   O Lamb of God, I come, I come.

6. Just as I am, thy love unknown
   Has broken ev'ry barrier down;
   Now to be thine, yea, thine alone,
   O Lamb of God, I come, I come.

East Wall Window

St. Peter

In Matthew 16:18, authority is given to the church to forgive sin in Jesus' name. Two keys represent dual authority, to open heaven to repentant sinners and to lock heaven to the unrepented. The inverted cross signifies Peter's concern that he not be killed in the same manner as Jesus, as he was not worthy, but rather hung upside down on the cross.

St. John

Son of Zebedee took part in the Last Supper and was the only one of the Twelve not to forsake the Savior in His hour of Passion. He denounced idol worship as demonic and wrote the Fourth Gospel, three Epistles, and possibly the Book of Revelation.

James the Less

Son of Alphaeus, and the same person as James "the younger" (Mark 15:40), may also be translated from the Greek, "the little" or "the less," which implies that he was shorter in stature than James, son of Zebedee.

St. Simon

Simon, meaning, "God has heard," and to distinguish him from St. Peter, is called Simon the Zealot, because he had a zeal for Jewish Law, which he practiced before his call.

St. James

The shells are symbols for pilgrimage and may be use as an emblem for saints known for their travels. James was the second recorded martyr in the New Testament.

St. Andrew

Always named among the first four apostles, this fisherman had been a disciple of John the Baptist. He became convinced that Jesus was the Messiah and brought his brother Peter to see Jesus.

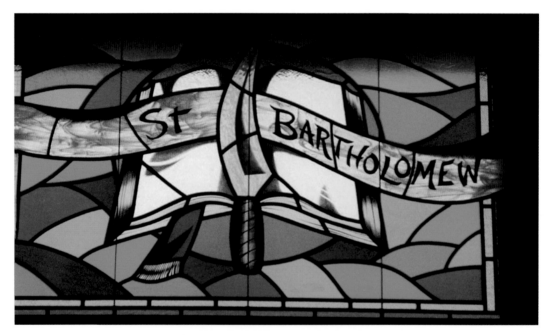

St. Bartholomew (Nathaniel)

Only mentioned once in the list of the Apostles in the New Testament, it is believed he preached the gospel in Ethiopia, India, Persia, and Armenia. In art, he is depicted holding a knife, an instrument of death.

St. Thomas

Named in all lists of the Twelve, Thomas insisted upon physical proofs of Jesus' resurrection, thus the label: "Doubting Thomas."

St. Philip

Called as Jesus' sixth disciple. In John 6:5-6, Philip is with Jesus at the Sea of Galilee during the miracle of Feeding the Five Thousand.

St. Matthew

One of the original disciples, and traditionally been identified as the author of the first Gospel in the New Testament. Matthew is mentioned twice as a tax collector.

St. Thaddaeus

Also known as Jude, he was the least known of the Apostles. He spoke only one time in the Gospels, at the Last Supper (John 14:22-23).

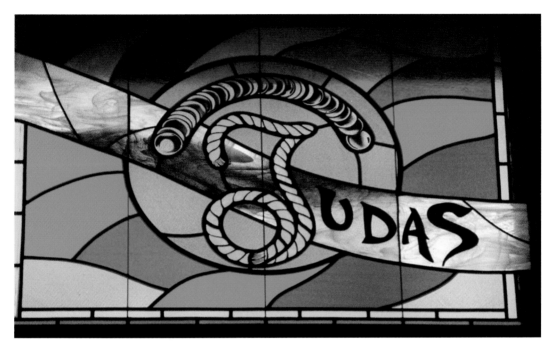

Judas

The treasurer of the original Twelve, he is known to betray Jesus. After Jesus' arrest, he was seized with remorse, returned the money, and hanged himself (Matthew 27:35). The 30 pieces of silver is symbolic of human greed.

Moses' Window

Creation Window

New Testament

Old Testament Prophets

Jesus' First Miracle

60

Feeding the Multitude

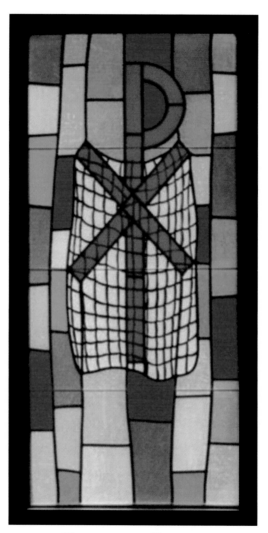

Calling of the Disciples

Old Testament Messianic Symbols

The symbols of the evangelists are taken from Ezekiel 1:10. The eagle, the winged lion, the winged man, and the winged ox are derived from Ezekiel's vision of the four living creatures.

St. Matthew

The winged man symbolizes St. Matthew because he began his gospel with the genealogy of Jesus.

St. Mark
The winged lion as clear proclamation of Jesus' Resurrection symbolizes St. Mark.

St. Luke

The ox is a symbol of strength, service, and patience. The symbol of St. Luke is the ox because of his emphasis on Jesus sacrificial atonement (Matthew 11:28-30).

St. John
The "soaring" witness to Jesus' divine nature is symbolized by the eagle.

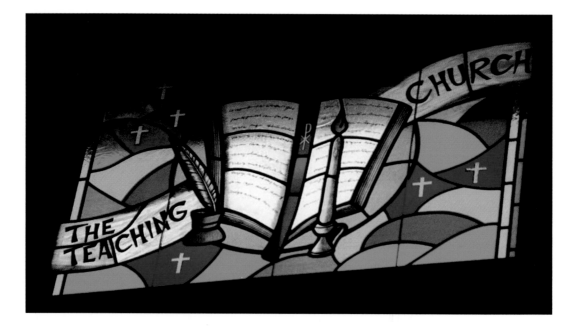

Lower Sanctuary Windows

Old Testament

The Moses Window

The cross shaped like the Greek letter T is referred to as the *Tau*. The Passover, which is the annual festival of the Jewish people, is recorded in Exodus 12:12-13 and commemorates the exodus from Egypt.

And the Lord said to Moses, "Make a poisonous serpent, and set it on a pole; and everyone who is bitten shall look at it and live" (Numbers 21:8). As the Israelites wandered in the wilderness, led by God, they became impatient and begin to grumble and rebel against God. Poisonous serpents came among the people, killing many, but at Moses' intercession the Lord made provision so that those bitten might live.

This imagery is later recorded in John 3:14-15, "And just as Moses lifted up the serpent in the wilderness, so must the Son of Man be lifted up, that whoever believes in him may have eternal life." In the New Testament passage, the symbol of the snake on a staff is symbolic of Jesus Christ, lifted upon a cross and crucified that we might live.

Mount Horeb, sometimes referred to as Mount Sinai, is called a holy mountain because it was the place where Moses met with God. This is where Moses caught sight of a bush that was on fire but not burning up. "When he approached the bush, God called Moses by name and then [God] said, 'Come no closer! Remove the sandals from your feet, for the place on which you are standing is holy ground.' He said further, 'I am the God of your father, the God of Abraham, the God of Isaac, and the God of Jacob.' And Moses hid his face, for he was afraid to look at God" (Exodus 3:5-6).

Reflection

The book of Exodus teaches us much about the holiness of God. Dr. Tony Everett, (Professor of Pastoral Care at Lutheran Theological Southern Seminary, Columbia, South Carolina) teaches the Holy Ground Model for theological reflection. In this model, the burning bush (Exodus 3:2) is discussed as "change in the normal that gets our attention." God speaks to us and reveals his presence to us through both the ordinary and the extraordinary. How have you recently stood on "holy ground"? Did you recognize the presence of God at that time, or was it only through later reflection that you realized the sacredness of your experience?

Hymns

When Israel Was In Egypt's Land (WOV #670)
(Let My People Go)

1. When Israel was in Egypt's land, let my people go;
   Oppressed so hard they could not stand, let my people go.
   Go down Moses, way down in Egypt's land,
   Tell old Pharaoh: let my people go.

6. Oh, let us all from bondage flee, let my people go;
And let us all in Christ be free, Let my people go.
Go down Moses, way down in Egypt's land,
Tell old pharaoh: let my people go.

Text: Psalm 136:1 (Latin); Taizé Community Music: Jacques Berthier, 1923-1994

Text and music © 1932, 1991 Les Presses de Taizé, SMIN. FI Publications, Inc.

The Creation Window

This window symbolizes God's role as the Creator and Ruler of all things. The hand of God (*Manus Dei*) is used as a symbol of God the Father. It was virtually the only symbol for God used during the first eight centuries of the church. The hand is symbolic of God's ownership of all creation and comes from the many references to the "hand of God" in the scriptures.

The images of the sun, moon, planets, plants describe in picture form the development of the universe from a "formless void" (Genesis 1:2), to a place where the Holy Spirit has moved to shape the chaos and bring the universe to life.

Later in the New Testament, the gospel of John begins with an echo of Genesis, "In the beginning was the Word and the Word was with God, and the Word was God ... All things came into being through him.... What has come into being in him was life, and the life was the light of all people" (John 1:1-4).

Reflection

God created every part of our world, from the miniscule to the monstrous. Bringing order out of chaos, God reveals his infinite power to us. As the scriptures unfold, the Holy Spirit enables us to see God's power to make all things new. He promises to restore our relationship with him, conquering sin, death, and the devil, so that we may spend eternity in the presence of the Triune God. What aspects of your life would you like to have recreated? What is in need of healing and newness of life?

Hymn

For The Beauty Of The Earth (LBW #561)

1. For the beauty of the earth, For the beauty of the skies,
   For the love which from our birth, over and around us lies:
   Christ, our Lord, to you we raise, this our sacrifice of praise.

2. For the wonder of each hour of the day and of the night,
   Hill and vale and tree and flow'r, Sun and moon and stars of light;
   Christ, our Lord, to you we raise, this our sacrifice of praise.

Old Testament Messianic Symbols Window

Throughout the Old Testament, there are multiple references to the coming of the Messiah, the Anointed One. God directed Moses that "a burning lamp [shall] be set to burn continually" (Exodus 27:20), symbolizing the continual presence of God with his people. Also associated with the scripture "thy word is a lamp to my feet and a light to my path" (Psalm 119:105). The spiritual darkness of gloom and despair will be driven away by Jesus Christ, the Light of the World.

The second symbol of the window is the monogram surrounded by the circle of eternity and set into the image of the sun. The IHC, is an older form of the first three letters of "Jesus" in Greek. The surrounding circle of eternity with the image of the sun artistically describes the Messianic name given to the Lord in Malachi 4:2, the Son of Righteousness.

In both the Old and New Testaments, the Messiah is compared to a lamb and in religious art, a lamb is an emblem of Christ. *Agnus Dei* (Latin, "Lamb of God") is shown as the Suffering Lamb with a cross and the Truimphal Lamb with a waving banner. The nimbus, a halo-like configuration surrounding the head of the lamb, is a sign of sanctity and light.

Reflection

The Messiah was anticipated for generations. Yet, when he came to earth in a humble birth, many did not recognize the Anointed One. How do our preconceived notions affect our ability to recognize the sacred amongst the ordinary?

Hymn

Agnus Dei (WOV #620)

> Lamb of God, you take away the sin of the world;
> Have mercy on us.
> Lamb of God, you take away the sin of the world;
> Have mercy on us.
> Lamb of God, you take away the sin of the world;
> Grant us peace.

Old Testament Prophets

The earliest writings of scripture were recorded on parchment or papyrus scrolls. The image of the scroll represents the Word of God. When it is included in the artistic image of a saint, it symbolizes the gift of writing. The artist's rendering includes a scroll and scepter, a sign of ruling authority.

God's unchanging and enduring nature is often represented as a rock. In the Old Testament, God was often spoken of as a rock. Messianic hopes in the Old Testament were tied to the cornerstone, which was later identified as Christ.

The image on the bottom represents a fiery chariot, when the prophet Elijah was taken up into heaven (2 Kings 2:1-11).

Reflection

All of the symbols of this window symbolize the strength of God and His constant power, passion, and compassion. His goodness endures forever. Of the three symbols, contemplate the one that has the most meaning to you. The symbols of God are a source of strength. How can you draw peace and hope from them?

Hymn

God Has Spoken By His Prophets (LBW #238)

   1. God has spoken by his prophets,
      Spoken his unchanging Word;

Each from age to age proclaiming God
The one, the righteous Lord.
In the world's despair and turmoil,
One firm anchor holds us fast:
God is king, his throne eternal;
God the first, and God the last.

2. God is speaking by his Spirit,
Speaking to the hearts of all,
In the ageless Word expounding
God's own message for us all.
Through the rise and fall of nations
One sure faith yet standing fast;
God abides, his Word unchanging;
God the first, and God the last.

Lower Sanctuary Windows

New Testament

Jesus' First Miracle Window

Webster's *New World Dictionary*, defines the term miracle as "an event or action that apparently contradicts known scientific laws." The symbolic significance of Jesus' miracles according to John is recorded in his gospel: "But these [signs] are written so that you may come to believe that Jesus is the Messiah, the Son of God, and that through believing you may have life in his name" (John 20:31).

The opening event in Jesus' ministry, the Marriage at Cana, (John 2:1-11), is only recorded in the gospel of John. Jesus performs this miracle in a personal setting, a wedding, before family and friends, showing that God is at work in the daily places of human lives. This miracle of new creation is also a sign of turning scarcity into abundance.

Jesus asks the servants to fill the stone jars with water. The containers in which the wine was created were used for Jewish rites of purification. The "water of Jewish law" now gives way to the joyful wine of the gospel!

Included in the stained-glass window is the symbol of marriage, the interlocking wedding rings, placed upon a Christ gram, from the Greek first letters of XP or Chi Rho. The two interlocking rings symbolize the unity of individuals whose unity is backed by Christ.

Reflection

Jesus' miracles are recorded in the New Testament and number over forty. Jesus performed miracles for two reasons: to relieve the suffering of people and to reveal God's power and might. Miracles happen many times in our lives, but often we miss experiencing them because of our own unbelief or lack of attentiveness. How does one stop, look, and listen to the ever-present, quiet Spirit? Think about the miracles that have taken place in your life. How has God led you through your life?

Hymn

Jesus, Come! For We Invite You (WOV #648)

1. Jesus, come! For we invite you,
   Guest and master, friend and Lord;
   Now, as one at Cana's wedding,
   Speak and let us hear your word:
   Lead us through our need and doubting,
   Hope be born and joy restored.

2. Jesus, come! transform our pleasures,
   Guide us into paths unknown;
   Bring your gifts, command your servants,
   Let us trust in you alone:
   Through your hand many work in secret,
   All shall see what you have done.

3. Jesus, come! in new creation,
   Heav'n brought near in pow'r divine;
   Give your unexpected glory,
   Changing water into wine:
   Rouse the faith of your disciples —
   Come, our first and greatest Sign

4. Jesus, come! surprise our dullness,
   Make us willing to receive more
   Than we can yet imagine,
   All the best to you have to give:
   Let us find your hidden riches,
   Taste your love, believe and live!

Feeding the Multitude Window

Jesus' fourth miracle, the feeding of the five thousand, is symbolized by the basket of five loves of bread and two fish. This is the only miracle that is recorded in all four of the gospels and it is the boldest, most public of the signs that Jesus performed.

Mark 6:30-44 describes how Jesus tried to give the twelve time for rest and share their stories, but the crowds would not let them have private time. Jesus had compassion for the crowd and possibly saw them as lost sheep, helpless and without a leader. He nourished their minds and souls with his teachings and then fed their bodies.

Although there were only five loaves of bread and two fish to share among them, there was enough for everyone. The simple foods of Jesus' day commonly included bread; it was so basic a staple that it became synonymous with life itself. "Give us each day our daily bread" (Luke 11:3) was a prayer for daily provision of food itself. In John 6:35, Jesus referred to himself as the "bread of life" because it was so basic, yet so critical — life giving.

Bread is to have been broken and not cut with a knife. Acts 20:7 states that "breaking bread was equivalent to having a meal." Fish was also a common food and many of the original twelve were fishermen by trade. The sign of the fish was a code by which the earliest Christians identified themselves to one another.

Reflection

We see the compassion, love, and hospitality of Jesus in this miracle. He cared deeply for the people gathered there as well as the people of today. Before distributing the food, he blessed the small quantity and gave thanks. In our lives are there times when we are short sighted and only see the present, but are later pleasantly surprised when there is more than enough. This miracle reveals to us that through Christ, out of scarcity, abundance is reaped.

Hymn

I Am The Bread Of Life (WOV #702)

1. "I am the Bread of life.
   You who come to me shall not hunger,
   And who believe in me shall not thirst.
   No one can come to me
   Unless the Father beckons"

2. "I am the resurrection,
   Flesh of the Son of Man and
   Drink of his blood, and
   Drink of his blood,
   You shall not have life with in you."

Refrain:
   "And I will raise you up,
   And I will raise you up,
   And I will raise you up on the last day."

The Calling of the Disciples

The stained-glass window rendering of the Calling of the Disciples depicts a fishing net draped over the Chi Rho.

"As [Jesus] walked by the Sea of Galilee, he saw two brothers, Simon, who was called Peter and Andrew, his brother, casting a net into the sea for they were fishermen. And he said to them, 'Follow me, and I will make you fish for people.' Immediately they left their nets and followed him" (Matthew 4:18-20).

It was not until the New Testament era that fishing developed, and then in the Sea of Galilee, Peter, Andrew, James, and John, partners in a fishing business, shared a viable industry. The cast net was circular in shape and measured about 15 feet in diameter, and was weighted at the edges with a long rope attached to the center. When a school of fish was seen in the water, the nets were dropped over them, the weights carried the net down and the fish were trapped beneath. When the day's fishing was completed, the nets were spread on the shore for drying and any broken pieces were mended.

The boats used for fishing were not normally very large. Two men could operate a boat and they often worked in partnership with another boat. When the disciples are listed by pairs, such as in Matthew 10:2-4, the pairs represent the way they sat in the boat and rowed together, as see from the position of Jesus who sat in the stern, "But he [Jesus] was in the stern" (Mark 5:38).

Reflection

Strong, well-mended equipment is necessary for a successful fishing trip. A guide or rudder is critical, whether in calm or turbulent waters. In our daily lives, how do we prepare ourselves for the tasks that are set before us? Remember the one who is at the stern is the one even the wind and the sea obey (Mark 4:41). How does Christ help us to navigate the storms in our lives? How do we recognize Jesus' presence within the still waters as well?

Hymn

They Cast Their Nets (LBW #449)

1. They cast their nets in Galilee,
   Just off the hills of brown;
   Such happy, simple fisherfolk,
   Before the Lord came down,
   Before the Lord came down.

2. Contented, peaceful fishermen,
   Before they ever knew
   The peace of God that filled their hearts
   Brimful, and broke them too,
   Brimful, and broke them too.

3. Young John, who trimmed the flapping sail
   Homeless in Patmos died.
   Peter, who hauled the teeming net,
   Head down the crucified,
   Head down the crucified.

4. The peace of God, it is no peace,
   But strife closed in the sod.
   Yet, let us pray for but one thing:
   The marv'lous peace of God,
   The marv'lous peace of God.

The Transfiguration Window

"Six days later, Jesus took with him Peter and James and John, and led them up a high mountain apart by themselves. And he was transfigured before them, and his clothes became a dazzling white, such as no one on earth could bleach them. And there appeared to them Elijah with Moses, who were talking with Jesus. Then Peter said to Jesus, 'Rabbi, it is good for us to be here; let us make three dwellings, one for you, one for Moses and one for Elijah.' He did not know what to say, for they were terrified. Then a cloud overshadowed them and from the cloud there came a voice, 'This is my Son, the Beloved; listen to him!' Suddenly when they looked around, they saw no one with them any more, but only Jesus" (Mark 9:2-8).

The accounts indicate that Jesus' face shone just as Moses' face did when he met God on Mount Sinai.

The most usual form of the Chi Rho consists of the P within the X and are the first two letters of the Greek word for Christ, which is an image in each of the New Testament stained-glass windows. Surrounding the Chi Rho are twelve flames significant of the twelve apostles or the twelve tribes of Israel.

On the left are two tablets, signifying the whole of God's law, the Pentateuch, which are the first five books of the Bible. The tablets also represent the Ten Commandments; three of them referring to people's relationship to God and the other seven addressing relationships among people.

The right side is the artist's rendering of the scrolls. Scrolls signify the writings of the gospels in the New Testament.

Reflection

Three of the gospels recount an extraordinary event in which Jesus takes three of his disciples up to a mountain and while they watch he is mystically "transfigured," as his physical presence was transformed and the two great prophets in Judaism, Moses and Elijah, stood beside him. It was one of only two times, the other being Jesus' baptism, in which a heavenly voice is heard in the gospels. The voice of God can be powerful or a gentle as a whisper. Do you listen for God's voice in your daily living? The Good News of Jesus Christ and His grace-filled love of His children is found repeatedly in the scriptures. How do you respond to His love and compassion for you?

Hymn

Shine, Jesus, Shine (WOV #651)

1. Lord, the light of your love is shining,
   In the midst of the darkness, shining;
   Jesus, light of the world, shine upon us,
   Set us free by the truth you now bring us.
   Shine on me, shine on me.

2. As we gaze on your kingly brightness,
   So our faces display your likeness,
   Ever changing from glory to glory,
   Mirrored here, may our lives tell your story,
   Shine on me, shine on me.

Refrain:
   Shine, Jesus, shine, fill this land with the Father's glory;
   Blaze, Spirit, blaze, set our hearts on fire.
   Flow, river, flow, flood the nations with love and mercy;
   Send forth your Word, Lord, and let there be light!

The Four Gospel-Etched Windows

Symbols of the Evangelists

The four window panels in the back of the sanctuary represent the authors of the canonical gospels: Matthew, Mark, Luke, and John. The four gospels that are grouped together in the New Testament were presumably written between 65-100 CE. The term "gospel" means "good news," which these writers proclaim through stories about the life and death of Jesus — his birth, ministry, miracles, teaching, last days, crucifixion, and resurrection. The imagery of the evangelists may be gleaned from Ezekiel (1:5-10; 10:19-22) and Revelation (4:7).

St. Matthew

Matthew, the tax collector (Matthew 9:9), may have been the author of the gospel bearing the same name, but scholars also question whether the writer deliberately chose to remain anonymous.

The gospel according to Matthew is comprised of three parts each one contains great speeches of Jesus:

    I. The presentation of Jesus (1:1—4:16)
   II. The ministry of Jesus to Israel (4:17—11:1)
  III. The journey of Jesus to Jerusalem and his suffering, death, and resurrection (16:21—28:20)

Since it is thought that Matthew's gospel is written more on the human side of Jesus and the other gospels, Matthew is usually pictured as a winged man.

St. Mark

Mark is the shortest of the four canonical gospels and the first to be written (between 65-75 CE). The first recorded comment on the gospel according to Mark was by a bishop named Papias, of the second century, in Hierapolis in Asia Minor. "Mark was the interpreter of Peter. He wrote down accurately, but without form, what he remembered of the things said and done by the Lord.... He had one thing in mind, namely to omit nothing of the things he had heard and to falsify nothing among them."

The author of Mark is a believer, as his gospel opens with the declaration that his text is the "good news of Jesus Christ, the Son of God" (Mark 1:1).

Mark's work is written in simple Greek, the ordinary language of the street, which is atypical for the literature of his time since the upper classes did most of the writing.

The author knows the scriptures of Israel, as they are quoted in some instances and referenced in others. He is also familiar with Jewish customs and beliefs, as he is very careful to distinguish various groups such as the Pharisees, Sadducees, and Herodians within the larger Jewish community.

Scholars believe that the gospel of Mark originally ended abruptly at 16:8; however, in a later attempt to conclude the text, scribes added verses 9-20 sometime after the fourth century CE. The possibility that the book was never completed or that it was damaged at an early stage has also been studied, but many researchers have ultimately concluded that the text ends appropriately for Mark — it is those who respond and follow the risen Lord who will see him.

The winged lion symbolizes St. Mark. The lion, as king of beasts, represents the royal character of Christ. Mark's emphasis on the resurrection parallels the meaning of an old fable: the cub of a lion who was born dead and after three days was licked to life by its father.

St. Luke

This book bears the name of Luke, "the beloved physician" of Colossians 4:14, and is generally identified as the third gospel. Because of its apparent inclusion of material from the gospel of Mark, scholars generally date it in the last third of the first century CE. Luke is the first volume of a two-part work, Luke-Acts, composed by the same author and dedicated to Theophilus. The name means "friend of God," and scholars are divided as to whether this was a name addressing Christians in general or a particular community.

The contents of the gospel may be summarized under eight headings:

    I.   Preface (Luke 1:1-4)
   II.   Infancy and childhood accounts (Luke 1:5—2:52)
  III.   The Galilean Ministry (Luke 4:14—9:50)
  IV.   The Journey to Jerusalem (Luke 9:51—19:28)
   V.   Travel to Jerusalem (Luke 9:51—19:28)
  VI.   Ministry in Jerusalem (Luke 19:29—21:38)
 VII.   The Passion Narrative (Luke 22:1—23:56)
VIII.   The Resurrection Narrative (Luke 24:1-53)

The heart of Luke's theology is an understanding of Jesus with the Holy Spirit being a very important theme.

It is only in Luke's gospel that Jesus' disciples ask him to teach them to pray (11:1). Luke portrays Jesus at prayer far more than any of the other gospels: nine times, as compared to five in Mark, three in Matthew, and two in John. Jesus also offers three parables on prayer in Luke that are not found anywhere else (11:5-8; 18:1-8, 9-14).

The ox, which depicts strength, service and patience, is used to symbolize St. Luke because of his emphasis on the sacrificial death of Jesus (Luke 22).

St. John

In John 20:30-31, John gives reasons for writing his gospel; he wants readers to see and hear that Jesus is the Christ and the Son of God. The book, perhaps written in a specific Christian community that was undergoing a painful separation from Jewish society, appears to have addressed the issue of maintaining belief rather than to convert outsiders.

It is in this gospel that Jesus makes some of his most familiar yet extraordinary declarations about himself. Jesus proclaims that he is "the bread of life" (6:35), "the light of the world" (8:12), "the good shepherd who lays down his life for his sheep" (10:11), and "the way, the truth, and the life" (14:6). Jesus also identifies himself as the Word of God "through whom all things were made." These sayings, deeds, and many more are found only in the fourth gospel.

The deeds done in the gospel of John are fewer in number, but for the most part, more spectacular. Jesus does nothing to hide his abilities; he performs miracles openly in order to demonstrate he is the Son of God.

In the fourth gospel, Jesus has come down from the Father and is soon to return to him. His message alone can bring eternal life. "I am the way, and the truth, and the life. No one comes to the Father except through me" (John 14:6).

The eagle symbolizes John's "soaring" witness to Jesus' divine nature.

Reflection

1. When you look at the windows, what common themes do you see?
2. Taking each separately, read the passage for each evangelist. Imagine what a tremendous responsibility it was for these four evangelists to see that their writings accurately captured their perceptions of the events of Jesus' life.
3. Do the etchings and other art forms help you to look at the scriptures in a different light?

Hymn

All Hail The Pow'r Of Jesus' Name! (LBW #328, 329)

1. All hail the pow'r of Jesus name!
   Let angels prostrate fall;
   Bring forth the royal diadem
   And crown him Lord of all,
   Bring forth the royal diadem
   And crown him Lord of all.

3. O seed of Israel's chosen race
   Now ransomed from the fall,
   Hail him who saves you by his grace
   And crown him Lord of all
   Hail him who saves you by his grace
   And crown him Lord of all.

4. Hail him, you heirs of David's line,
   Whom David Lord did call —
   The God Incarnate, man divine —
   And crown him Lord of All,
   The God Incarnate, man divine —
   And crown him Lord of all.

Reformation Windows

The four stained-glass windows in the narthex (commons area) represent the Reformation Era. The windows, designed by Patti Lloyd, former member of Cross and Crown, depict four Lutheran Reformation themes.

Over 400 years ago, a German monk and professor of theology named Martin Luther (1483-1546) challenged the practice of buying one's way into heaven through the purchase of indulgences, letters purchased to assure people of forgiveness and salvation in this world and in the hereafter. Over the centuries, these indulgence letters had arisen to make penance more tolerable, but they had also come to be used to raise money for special projects like the building of St. Peter's Basilica in Rome.

Luther's motivation came from the biblical truth that "the just shall live by faith" in order to inherit eternal life with God. The center of this evangelical theology was the certainty of God's forgiveness to those who repent of their sin and trust in Jesus Christ alone as the way of salvation. Luther did not regard this belief as a new theology, but as the recovery of the gospel message for a church that had lost its center. The recovery of that center — and the assurance and comfort it brings — was the goal of the Reformation and its theology (Romans 3:21-26; 4:5).

Luther's revelation of the grace of God has left an undeniable mark on the history of the world.

The Reforming Church Window
In order to protect people from the deception of the indulgences, Luther wrote in Latin 95 theses, which, among other things, debated the power of indulgences and the pope's right to offer them. These were posted on the door of the Castle Church in Wittenberg, Germany, and were also sent to the highest church officials in Germany. Later, the theses were translated into German, the language of the people.

In his *Ninety-five Theses* Luther asserts:

1. When our Lord and Master Jesus Christ said, "Repent" (Matthew 4:17), he willed the entire life of believers to be one of repentance.

27. They preach only human doctrines that say that as soon as the money clinks into the money chest, the soul flies out of purgatory.

36. Any truly repentant Christian has a right to full remission of penalty and guilt, even without indulgence letters.

43. Christians are to be taught that he who gives to the poor or lends to the needy does a better deed than he who buys indulgences.

62. The true treasure of the church is the most holy gospel of the glory and grace of God.

Luther wanted to drive out the practice of selling indulgences in much the same way as Jesus drove the moneychangers out of the temple (Mark 11:15-17). Luther's actions triggered immense unrest throughout Germany. However, he did not set out to begin a new church rather, he wanted to reform the Catholic church by debating those whose teachings he thought were hindering the Living Word. Luther's ultimate goal was to teach and preach the unadulterated gospel.

Luther wanted the church to remain united, but when division seemed imminent, the *Augsburg Confession*, a statement expressing the reformer's position, was brought before the Papal Party in 1530. Articles 22-28 list seven changes that the sixteenth-century reformers wanted:

22. Lay persons are to receive both the bread and wine in the Sacrament.
23. Priests are allowed to marry.
24. Mass is restored as a communion rather than a good work.
25. Emphasis in confession is on absolution rather than on the listing of sins.
26. Fasting and other disciplines are encouraged but not as ways of earning salvation.
27. The vows of monks and nuns are not binding if made for improper reasons.
28. Bishops are no longer to rule as "worldly powers."

Authored by Martin Luther's associate, Philipp Melanchthon, the confession failed to accomplish its purpose — to preserve the unity of the Western church. Consequently, the reformers were forced to form their own organization outside the Roman Catholic church that came to be known as the "Lutheran" or "Evangelical" Church.

The task of living as a reforming movement continues today. The Holy Spirit continually moves within our midst, calling us and leading us to live Christ-centered lives in a secular world. Luther's courage to respond to God's call by challenging the powerful structure of the Roman Catholic church continues to inspire us as twenty-first-century disciples of Christ and reformers of the church.

The Singing Church Window

Martin Luther stands apart from the reformers of his day in affirming music as an excellent gift of God to be used to praise him and proclaim his Word. Only Luther unhesitatingly commended the use of music for the nourishment of the Christian life and in the worship of the church.

Luther has been quoted: "We can mention only one point (which experience confirms), namely that next to the Word of God, music deserves the highest praise." Luther came to understand through his own personal experience the exceptional power of music to move the hearts and minds of people.

From such a perspective, he encouraged the teaching and singing of both the most sophisticated musical forms of his day as well as the simpler congregational hymns. The Calvinist Reformation excluded art and music of any kind in public worship, allowing only a simple congregational psalmody. In contrast, Luther encouraged and actively fostered the practice of congregational singing as well as performed music in Christian life and worship. From this emphasis, a sacred music tradition of great richness and depth was born.

Luther's concern that pastors and teachers were musically trained as well as his collaboration with musicians in the preparation of music for the liturgy had a direct and crucially important role in the life and worship of the church.

For Martin Luther there were five understandings or "paradigms of praise":

I. Luther strongly believed that *music was a creation and a gift of God*.

II. Music in the church was intended for a specific purpose: "The praise of the Creator and proclamation of grateful thanks for the redemption won for the world in Jesus Christ."

III. Music had a clear role in corporate worship, and the liturgy was to be sung, no matter how modest the musical resources might be. Another great contribution of the Lutheran reformation was the restoration of congregational singing. For Luther, the congregational hymn was a tool for involving the faithful in the singing of the liturgy.

IV. Luther understood active congregational participation in worship as a necessary consequence of the doctrine of the royal priesthood of all believers. His concern was that the faithful not only be present at the worship, but that they also become active participants. Praise, proclamation, and adoration were to involve the whole people of God, rather than being the sole responsibility of the leaders, choirs, and preachers in the worship service.

V. Luther viewed continuity with the practice of the whole church to be an important factor in shaping the music and worship of God's people. During the Reformation movement, Luther sought to uplift and retain all that was good in reference to the liturgical practices and revise or eliminate only those practices that conflicted with his understanding of the Gospel. To accept those gifts of tradition was, for Luther, to be linked with Christians of other times and places and to be reminded that the church of his day was indeed part of the one, holy, catholic and apostolic company of saints.

Martin Luther's contributions to the music of the church, by writing musical scores and texts, are far reaching. In December 1523, Luther's *Order of Mass and Communion* appeared in print. In early January of the year 1524 a Nurnberg printer, Jobst Gutknecht, had begun to compile into a hymnal a series of hymns that he had obtained through a third person. In the sixteenth century there were no copyright laws and a printer was free to print anything. This oldest Lutheran hymnal is known as the *Achtliederbuch* (*Hymnal of Eight*), and contains four hymns by Luther: "Dear Christians, Let Us Now Rejoice," "Ah God, From Heaven Look Down," "Although The Fools Say With Their Mouth," and "From Troubled Deep I Cry To Thee."

The first hymnal prepared under Luther's own auspices is the *Geistliche Gesandbuchlein*, published in Wittenberg in 1524. This was primarily designed not for the congregation but for the choir. This kept with Luther's thoughts that he wanted his hymns to be sung by the choir to familiarize the whole congregation with them. More than two-thirds of Luther's hymns were written between the late fall of 1523 and the summer of 1524.

During the Reformation, close to 100 of the 1,524 hymnals were produced until Luther's death in 1546. In 1527, he wrote the best-known hymn of the Reformation, "A Mighty Fortress Is Our God" (based on Psalm 46, with music written by Luther's friend Johann Walter). "I would like to see all the arts, especially music, used in the service of the One who created them and gave them to us," said Luther. "If I had my way, children would learn not only languages and history but also singing and music."

The Teaching Window

Luther was concerned not only about Christian education but about education in general. He urged that good education be given to all so that the well-educated could serve God and neighbor in their occupations and also so that the church could have well-educated clergy.

The following is Luther's Blueprint for Educational Reform (see page 116):

"Good God, what wretchedness I beheld! The common people, especially those living in the country have no knowledge whatever of Christian teaching, and unfortunately many pastors are quite incompetent and unfitted for teaching. Although the people are supposed to be Christian, are baptized, and receive the holy sacrament, they do not know the Lord's Prayer, the Creed, or the Ten Commandments." (*The Small Catechism*, Preface)

Luther had stressed the necessity of catechetical instruction since the beginning of the Reformation. He published his explanations to the chief parts of the Christian faith and they were produced on individual sheets and sold for a few pennies each. By the middle of 1529, printers in Wittenberg collected them into what they called an *enchiridion* or handbook. Luther added a preface and by the end of the same year the printers had given the handbook a subtitle by which we know it today, *The Small Catechism of Martin Luther*.

When each individual part of *The Small Catechism* was sold separately, each sheet had its own heading: "... in a simple way in which the head of a house is to present them to the household." Luther wrote *The Small Catechism* for the home, so that parents could explain to their children in simple terms the most important things in the Christian faith. For Luther, the household is a house church.

There are sections for morning and evening prayers and prayers before and after mealtimes. There is an entire section in which Luther uses Bible verses to describe how we are to behave toward one another as parents, children, married people, and workers. Also included are the services of Marriage and Holy Baptism: in Luther's day, marriage was the time when households came into being and baptism begins the life of faith for all Christians.

The five chief parts of *The Small Catechism* have their place in worship. The Ten Commandments and Confession prepare us for confession and forgiveness. The Apostles' Creed and Lord's Prayer are used in worship. Holy Baptism and Communion are two sacraments that create the Christian church.

The original printings of *The Small Catechism* included artwork. These illustrations were woodcuts: there was one illustration based on a biblical story for each commandment, article of the Creed, petition for the Lord's Prayer and sacrament.

The "German Catechism," later called the *Large Catechism* was published in April 1529. This doctrinal textbook, written for clergy, was a summary of the Christian faith as Luther perceived it. It was his understanding of the gospel as the source of a new life liberating man from sin, death, and the devil. The background material for the *Large Catechism* was taken from three series of sermons that Luther preached in 1528 and 1529. Later that same year, Luther issued a revised edition that added an "Exhortation to Confession," a lengthy insertion in the introduction to the explanation of the Lord's Prayer and several marginal notes. This edition was the first to be illustrated.

Luther was also very concerned about placing the scriptures into the hands of the people. He thought if he could translate the scriptures into the language of the people and place a guide to reading and understanding them into the hands of every Christian, then everyone could become *theodidacti*, people taught by God. Luther translated the entire New Testament into German within eleven weeks, working at the rate of more than 1,500 words per day. In doing so, he took great care to use the language of the people. During the midst of the work he said, "I have undertaken to translate the Bible into German. This was good for me; otherwise I might have died in the mistaken notion that I was a learned fellow." Together with his colleagues, Luther spent the rest of his life preparing and refining both testaments of his German Bible.

Martin Luther's Seal
Martin Luther wrote this explanation of his seal in a letter penned at Colburg Castle, which was sent to Lazarus Spengler on July 8, 1530.

"Since you wish to know whether my seal is well done, I shall gladly comply with your request by communicating to you the thoughts I originally desired my seal to embrace as indicative of my theology.

"First there is a cross, black on a heart in red, as its natural color. This is to remind me that faith in the Crucified saves us; for one believes with the heart, one is justified. Now although it is a black cross, although it mortifies and is designed to inflict pain, it nonetheless allows the heart to keep its color, it does not destroy its nature, that is, it does not kill but keeps alive. (For the just lives by faith, but faith in the Crucified.)

"Such a heart is to be centered on a white rose in order to indicate that faith yields joy, comfort, and peace and straightway beds one on a white pleasing rose. Nor does faith yield the peace and joy of the world. Therefore the rose would be white and not red, because white is the color of the spirits and of all the angels.

"This rose is on a field tinted with the hues of heaven to indicate that this joy in the spirit and faith is a beginning of the future heavenly joy, a joy which, to be sure, is even now present in faith and embraced by hope but is not yet revealed.

"Around this field runs a ring of gold to show that the blessedness of heaven endures forever and ever and is more precious than all pleasures and possessions of earth, as gold is the most precious and the noblest metal."

Reflection

The Holy Spirit continually moves within our midst calling us and leading us to live Christ-centered lives in a largely secular world. Luther's courage to respond to God's call by challenging the powerful structure of the Roman Catholic church continues to inspire us as disciples of Christ and reformers of the church. The Reformation windows and Martin Luther's Seal are artistic symbols of our Lutheran heritage and beliefs. How do the windows bring to mind feelings of faith? Are the symbols as significant today as in Luther's time? Are there expressions of our Lutheran heritage today? Martin Luther passed this heritage on through writings, teaching, preaching, art, and music. How will we pass on our heritage to future generations?

Hymn

Lord, Keep Us Steadfast in Your Word (LBW #230)

1. Lord, keep us steadfast in your Word:
   Curb those who by deceit or sword
   Would wrest the kingdom from your Son
   And bring to naught all he has done

2. Lord Jesus Christ, your pow'r make known,
   For you are Lord of Lords alone;
   Defend your holy Church, that we
   May sing your praise triumphantly.

3. O Comforter of priceless worth,
   Send peace and unity on earth;
   Support us in our final strife
   And Lead us out of death to life.

West Wall Window
The final window that will be reflected upon is one that may one day be incorporated into the narthex (common area) architecture. This window is a mirror of the window above the altar on the East Wall, which symbolizes our Christianity by depicting the birth and resurrection of Jesus Christ and the two sacraments of the Lutheran church: Baptism and Holy Communion.

"Go in peace and serve the Lord" is a sending that the congregation hears and responds to every Sunday with "Thanks be to God!" But what does that really mean in our daily lives as we leave the building and go forth into the world? The East Wall window shows us how God meets us through the Good News and it reveals to us the peace that surpasses all understanding. (The way to the Good News and the peace that our spirit needs. Spirit is a word for breath, wind, and life.) God sets us free from the bondage of sin through the gifts of Baptism and Communion, and through these gifts, God heals our spirit. The wind and the life of our being changes; as children of God, we have peace with our own existence and purpose. Our bodies and minds may also be words for house, structure, and form. Harmony between your house and your spirit is a gift from God that enables us to reach out to others with compassion and love. Together, here at Cross and Crown, the Holy Spirit is enabling us to create a healing peace through the Word, Prayer, Sacraments, and Service.

Hymn

The Lord Now Sends Us Forth (LBW #538)

> The Lord now sends us forth with hands to serve and give,
> to make of all the earth a better place to live.
> The angels are not sent into our world of pain
> to do what we were meant to do in Jesus' name;
> that falls to you and me and all who are made free.
> Help us, O Lord, we pray, to do your will today.

Window Donations

Old Testament:

The Moses Window (Burning Bush, Tau Cross)
Harry and Judy Williams

The Creation Window (Hand of God, Rising Sun)
Evelyn Lageman and children Robert, James, Janet

Old Testament Messianic Symbols (The Lamp, The Lamb, The Sun)
Gerald and Claudia Jo Zapka

Old Testament Prophets (Scroll, Stones, and Wheel)
David and Lynn Wallin

New Testament:

Jesus' First Miracle (Water Jars and Symbols for Marriage)
Fran Hoke

Feeding the Multitude (Loaves and Fishes)
Joe and Evelyn Bookout

The Calling of the Disciples (Net and Chi Rho)
The Kasting Family

The Transfiguration (Stone tablets, Chi Rho, and scroll)
John and Elizabeth Lingel Kasting

East Wall Window:

William A. Weaver
Mr. and Mrs. D.A. Ellison
Bobby Weber

Rick and Kim Glackin
Frank Macarine Family
Mary Lib and Chris Whalen
Dr. and Mrs. Harold Hoke

The Clerestory Windows:

Fred Hahn Jr. and Family
Lyn Porter
Hugh Kluttz Jr. and Susan Blair-Kluttz
Ike and Virginia Wagner
Evelyn and Joe Bookout
Friends of Clara and Fred Hahn
The Westendorffs
The Sensenbrenners
Edith Tarleton
Ellen Keller

Reformation Windows:

Gifts and Memorials

Narthex Etched Window:

Ate and Vern Fransen
Tom and Mary Anne Alexander
Jean Rhodes
Peter Murrill Family

Glossary

Alpha and Omega — Signifies Jesus Christ, "The first and the last, the beginning and the end" (Revelation 22:13); "the same yesterday and today and forever" (Hebrews 13:8)

Altar — in Christian churches, the symbol of Christ's sacrificial death; it is an everlasting symbol of his spiritual presence in the church and also reminds us of the table in the Upper Room where the Lord's Supper was instituted

Chi Rho — derived from the first two letters of the Greek word XPICTOC (*Christos*), is an ancient monogram of Christ, being used for at least 1,600 years

Clerestory — the part of the church building that is higher than the roofs of the other parts of the building and usually contains windows

East Wall — the wall area behind the altar. In the early church the belief was that the source of all life was from the east. Just as the rising of the sun announces new life for the day, so the basis for all life comes from the east. Also as a sign that the church was prepared for the second coming of Christ, altars were set on the east wall of the building, so when the faithful prayed they would face in the direction of the coming of the Lord. In churches of today, whether the altar is built close to the east wall or not, the wall behind the altar is referred to as the East Wall.

Resources

Rest, Friedrich, *Our Christian Symbols*. The Pilgrim Press, Cleveland, Ohio

Klein, Patricia S., *Worship Without Words — The Signs and Symbols of Our Faith*. Paraclete Press, Brewster, Massachusetts

Hall, Sarah, *The Color of Light — Commissioning Stained Glass for a Church*. Liturgy Training Publications, Chicago, Illinois

Bangert, Mark, *Symbols and Terms of the Church*. Augsburg Fortress, Minneapolis, Minnesota

Knowles, Andrew, *The Bible Guide*. Augsburg Fortress, Minneapolis, Minnesota

Lockyer, Herbert, *All the Apostles of the Bible*. Zondervan, Grand Rapids, Michigan

LBW — Lutheran Book of Worship

Narthex or commons area — the name given to the gathering space between the outside door of the church and the sanctuary

Nave — the long body of the church

Pulpit — a piece of furniture which upholds the Word of God, and where preaching, scripture reading, and prayers are offered

Sanctuary — meaning sacred or holy place

Synoptic Gospels — the New Testament books of Matthew, Mark, and Luke

WOV — Lutheran Hymnal, With One Voice

ELW — Evangelical Lutheran Worship

_____

(from page 105)

In 1527, due to peasant uprisings and tensions between radical and conservative Lutherans, Martin Luther wrote guidelines for a program of visitations to congregations, "Articles of Visitation." In Saxony and later in Hesse, visitation teams consisting of four members were sent to examine economic conditions and to evaluate religious affairs.

About the Author

Elaine Koenig Krome is a native of North Dakota and a graduate of Lutheran Theological Southern Seminary with a Master of Arts in Religion. As an Associate in Ministry of the Evangelical Lutheran Church in America, she serves as the Coordinator for the Lutheran Association of Christian Educators. Elaine and her husband, Ron, are former members of Cross and Crown Lutheran Church, Matthews, North Carolina. Currently, they reside in Bluffton, South Carolina, and are members of Lord of Life Lutheran Church. They have two grown sons.